EXTREME DOT PUZZLES WITH OVER 15000 DOTS

DOT TO DOT PUZZLE

BY **MODERN PUZZLES PRESS**

CITIES AND FAMOUS PLACES AROUND THE WORLD

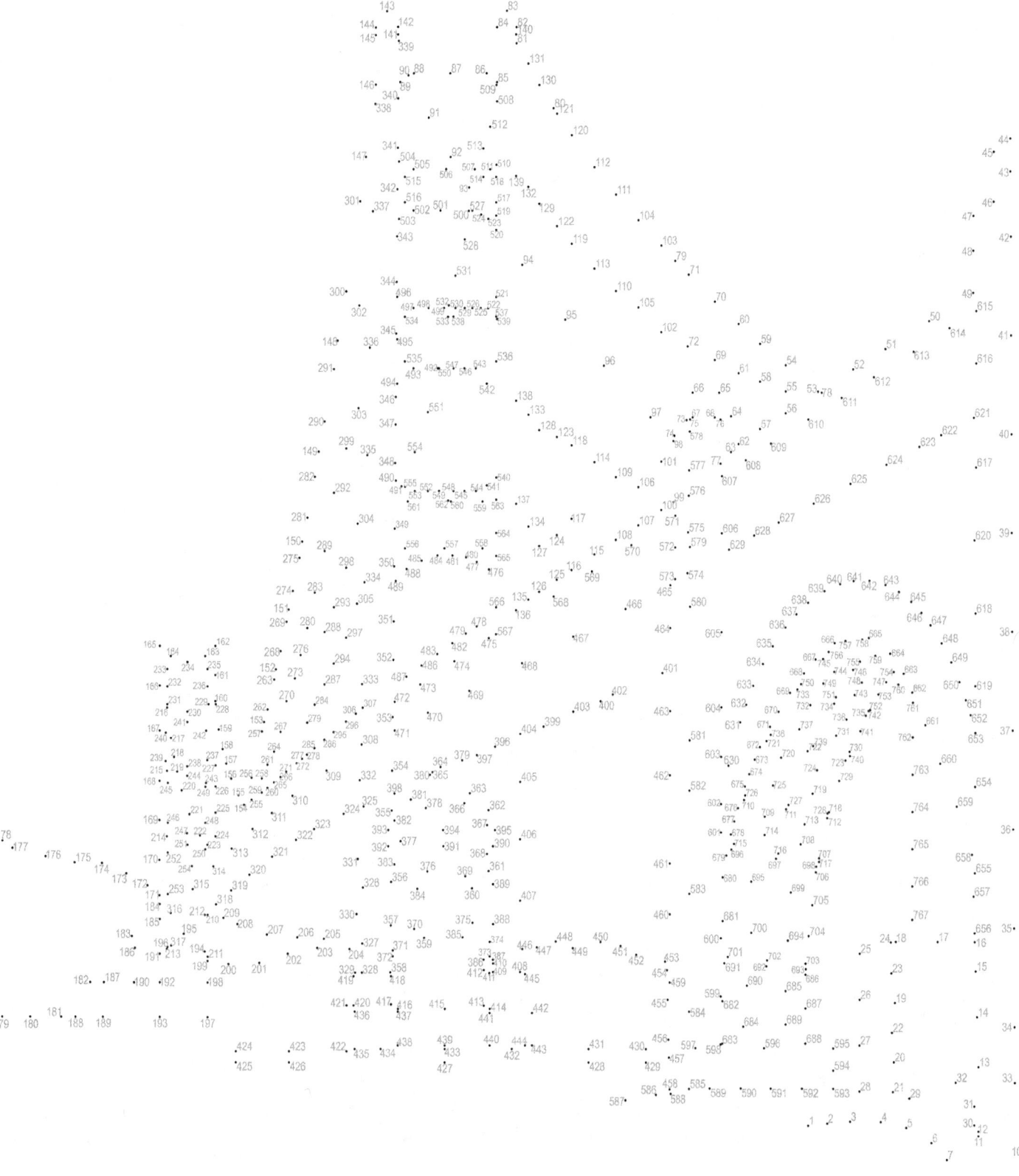

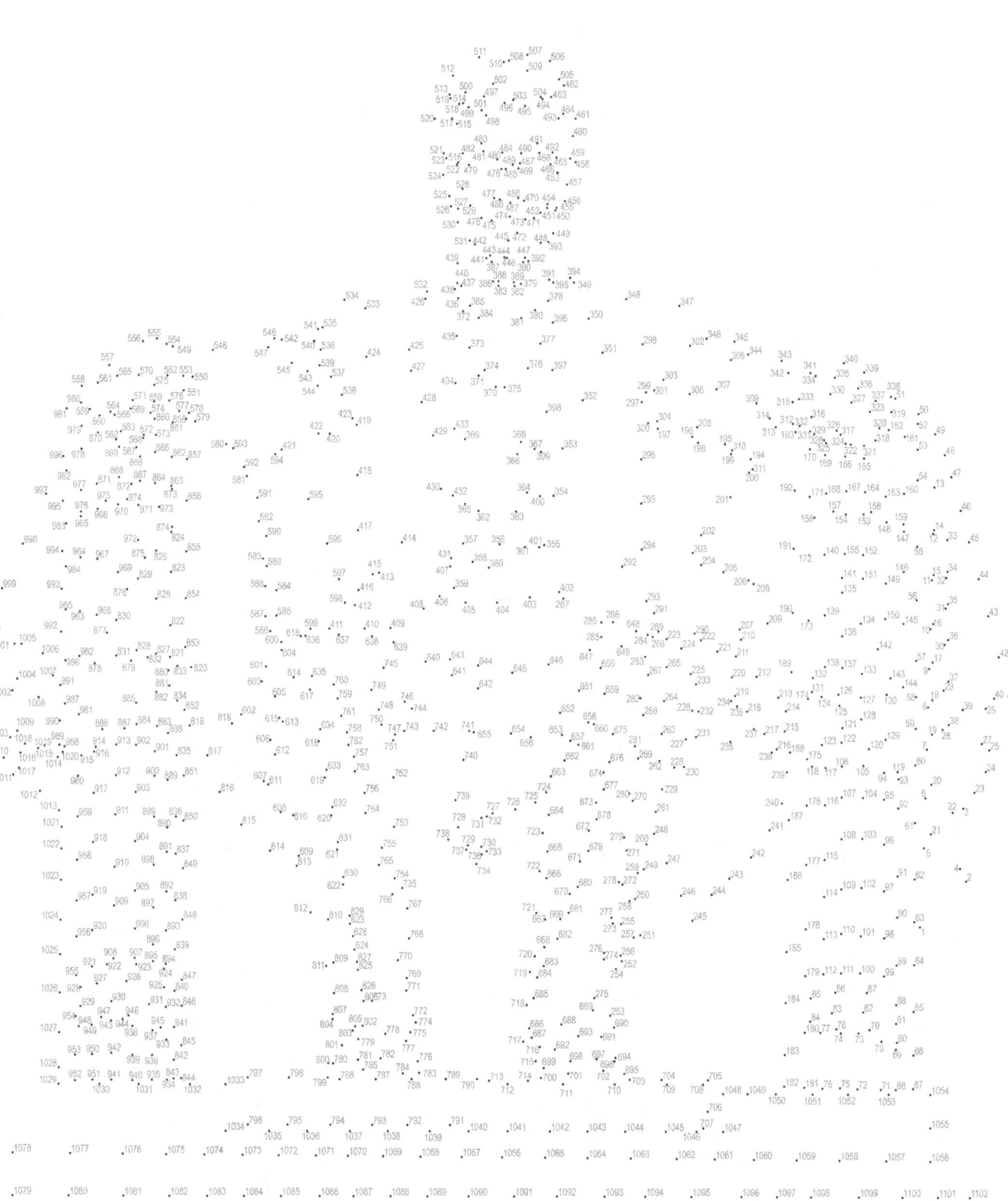

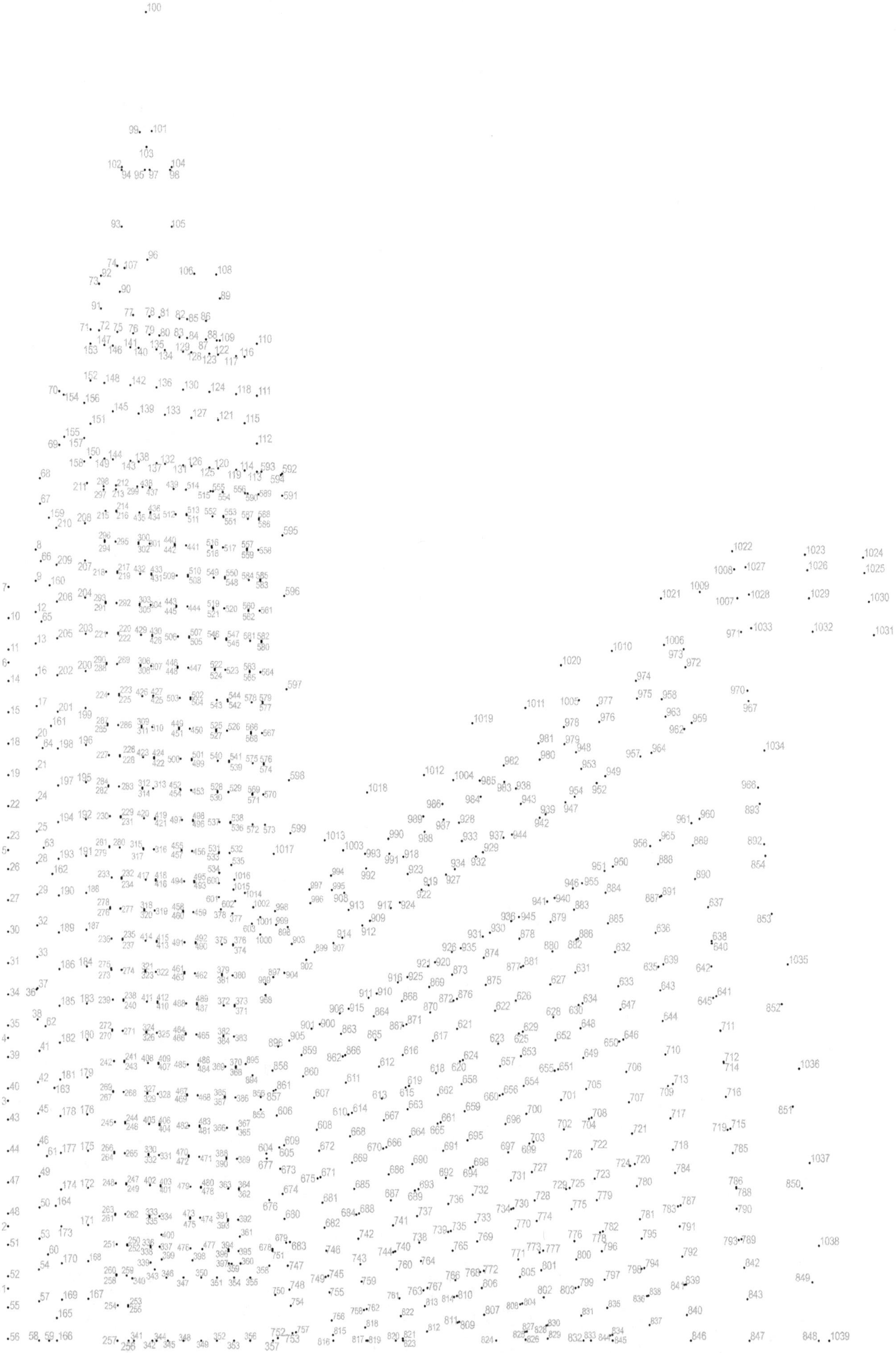

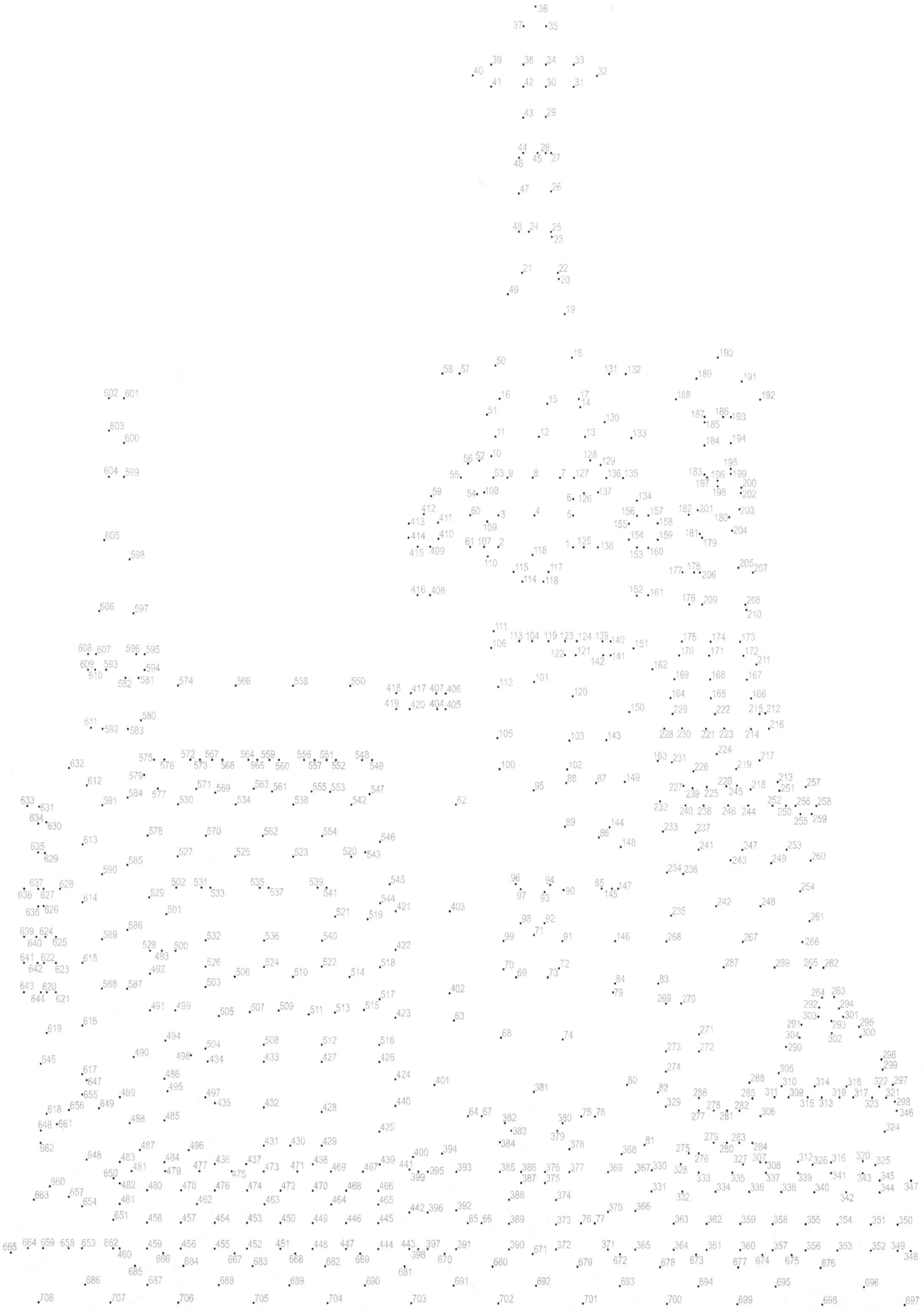

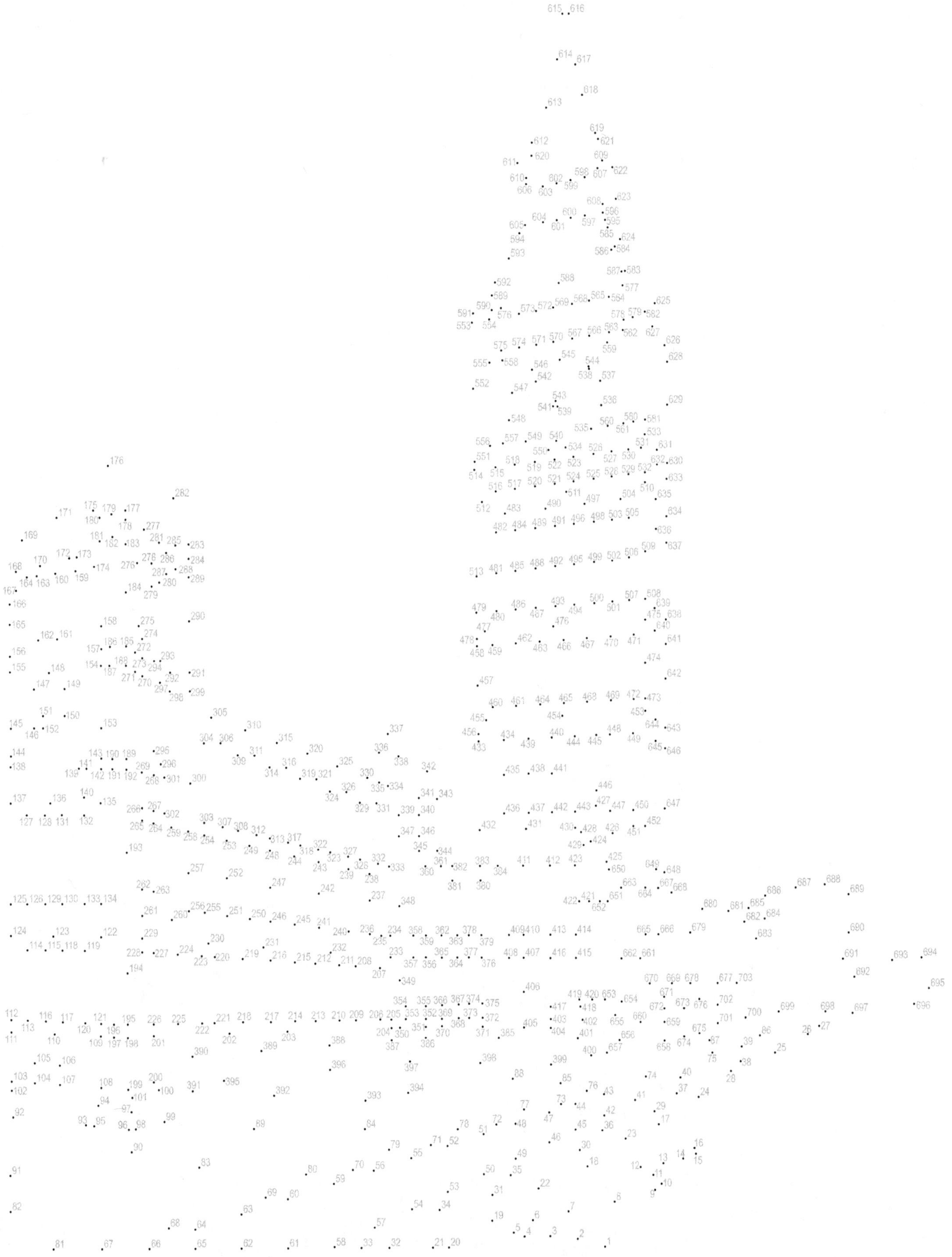

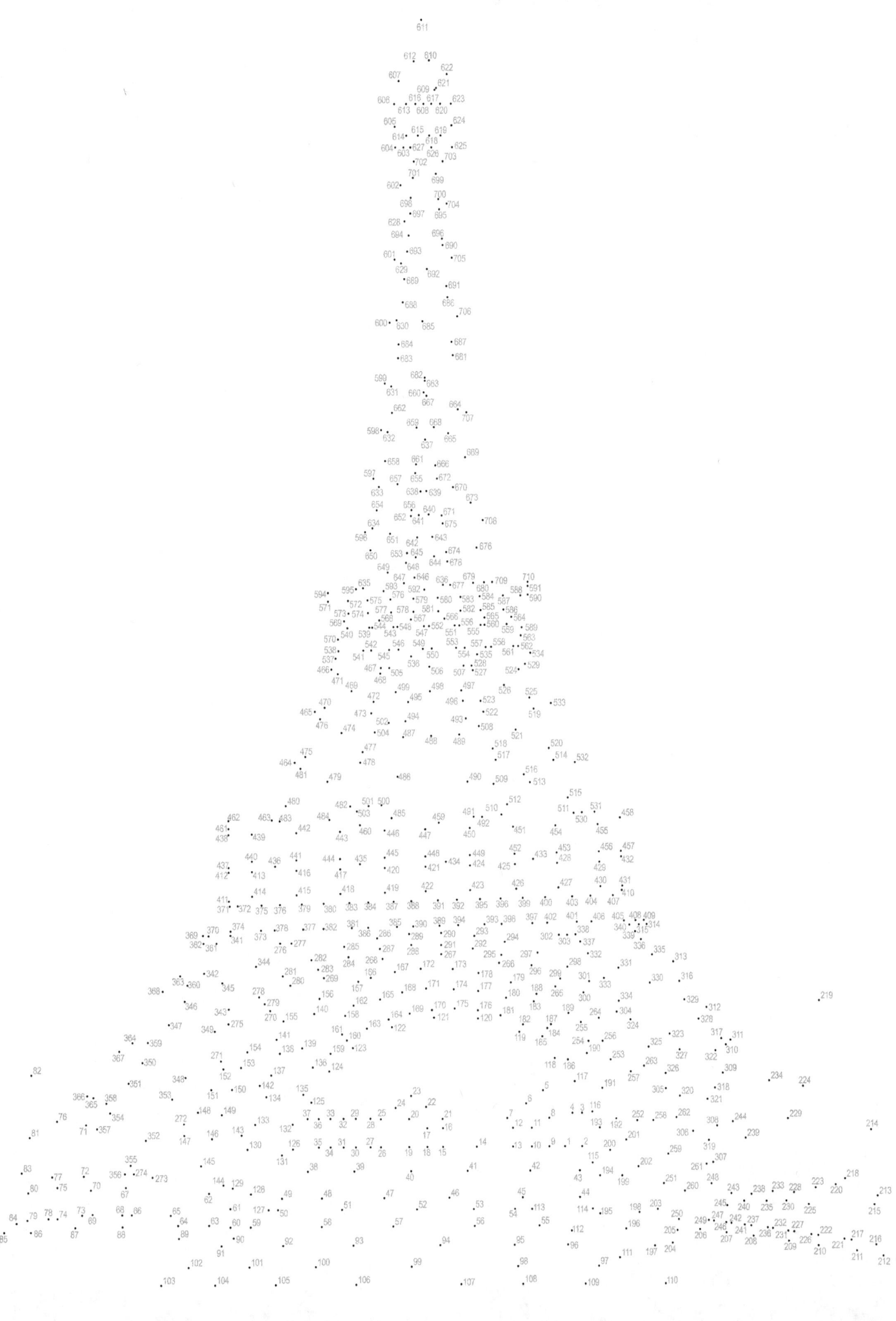

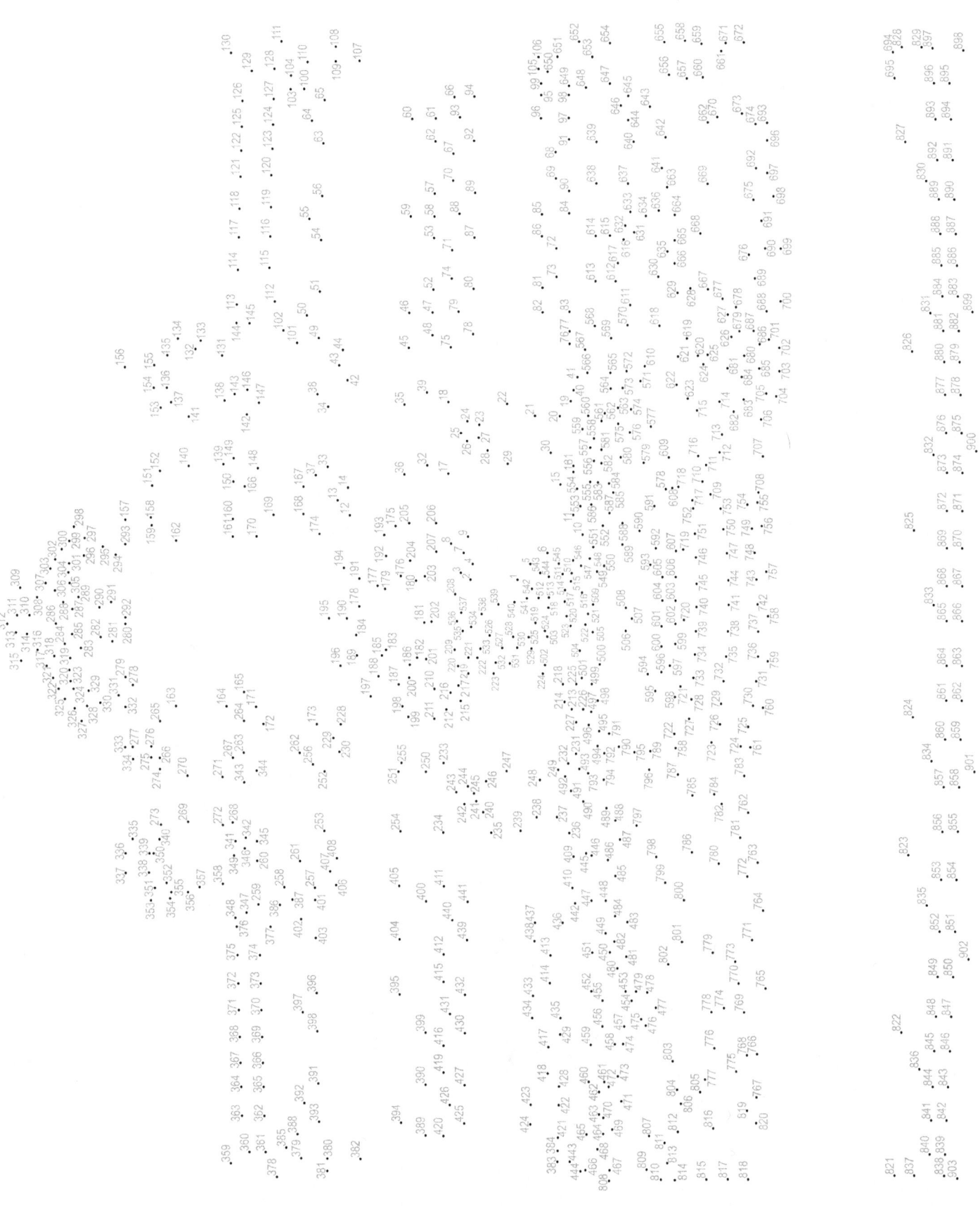

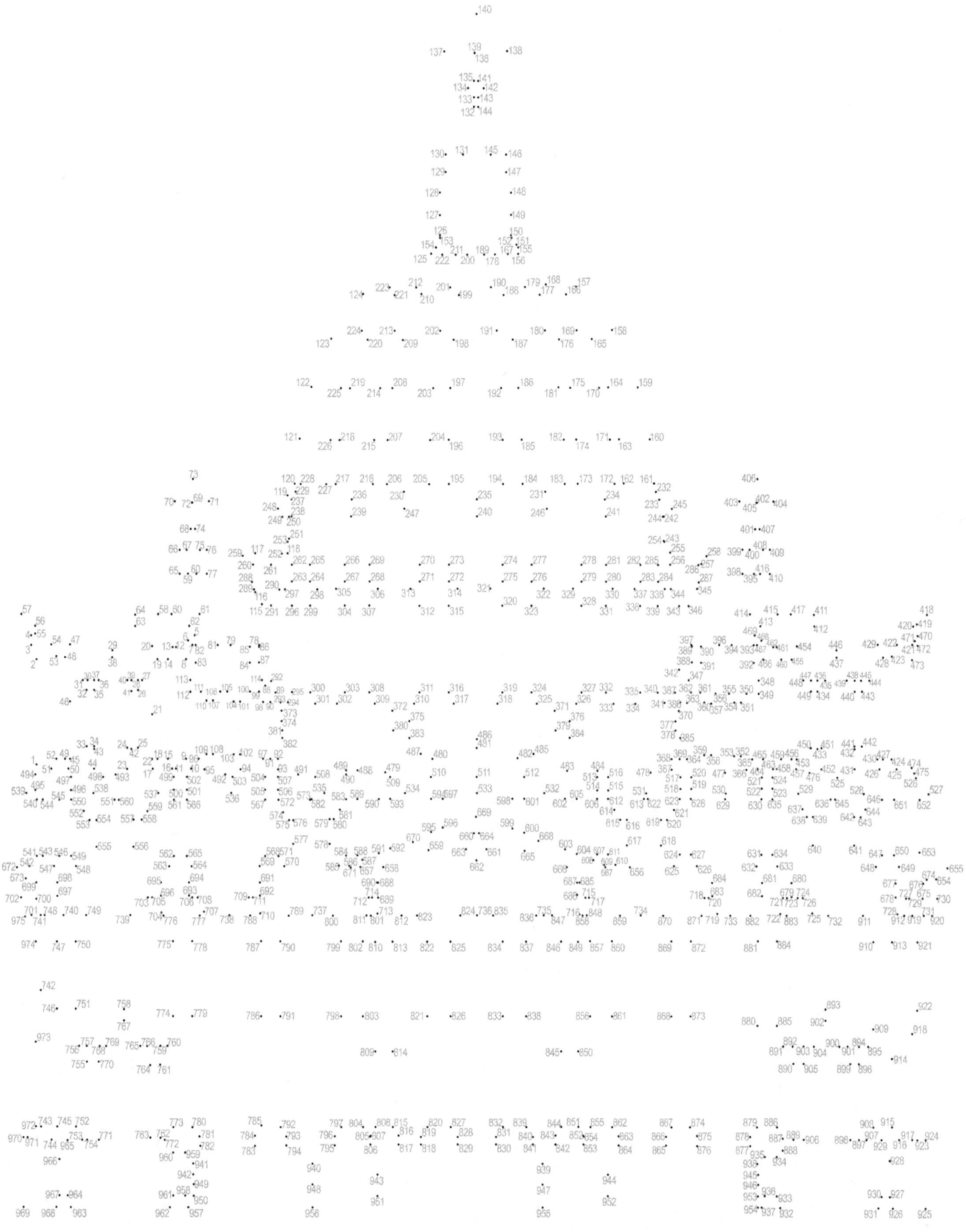

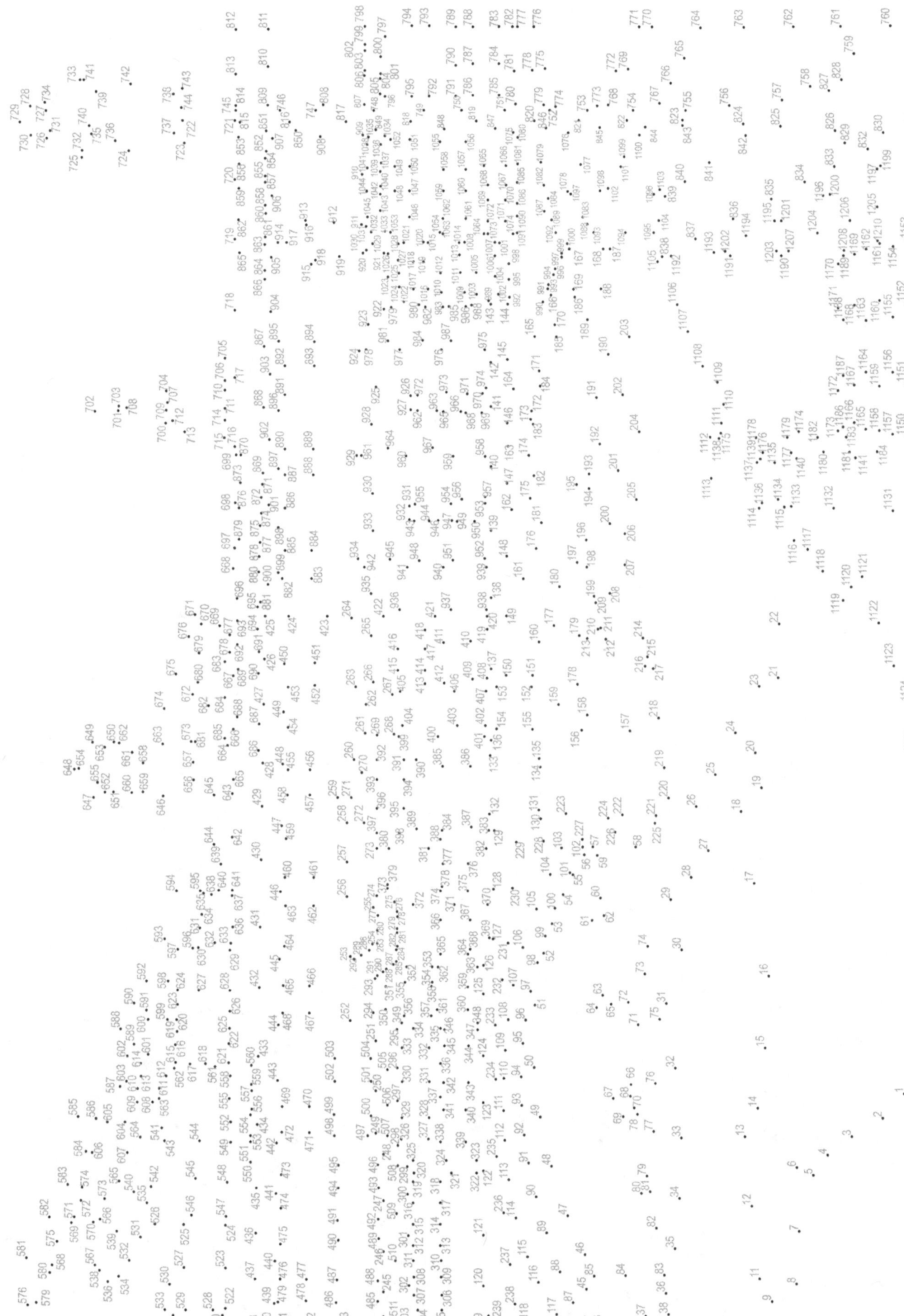

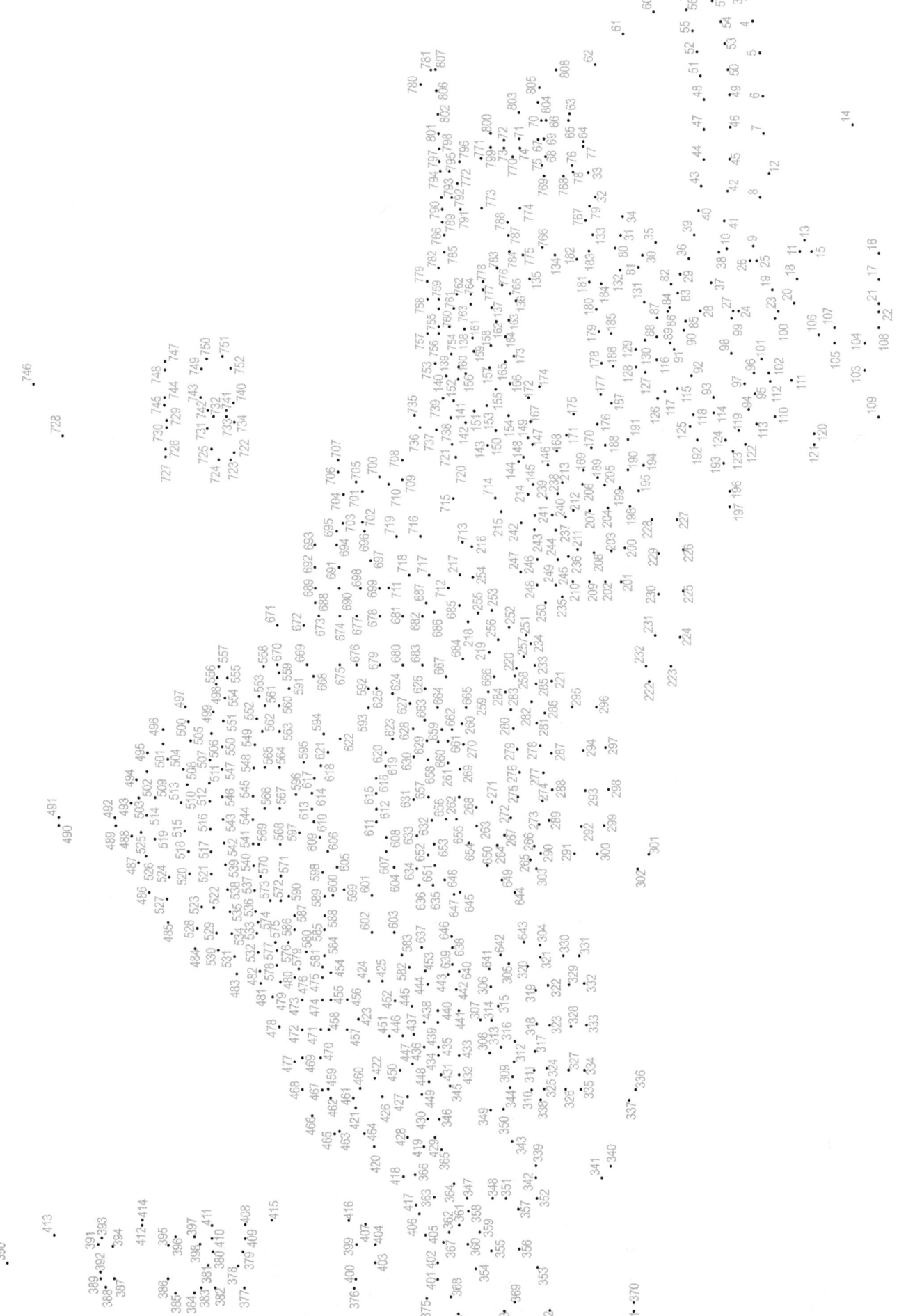

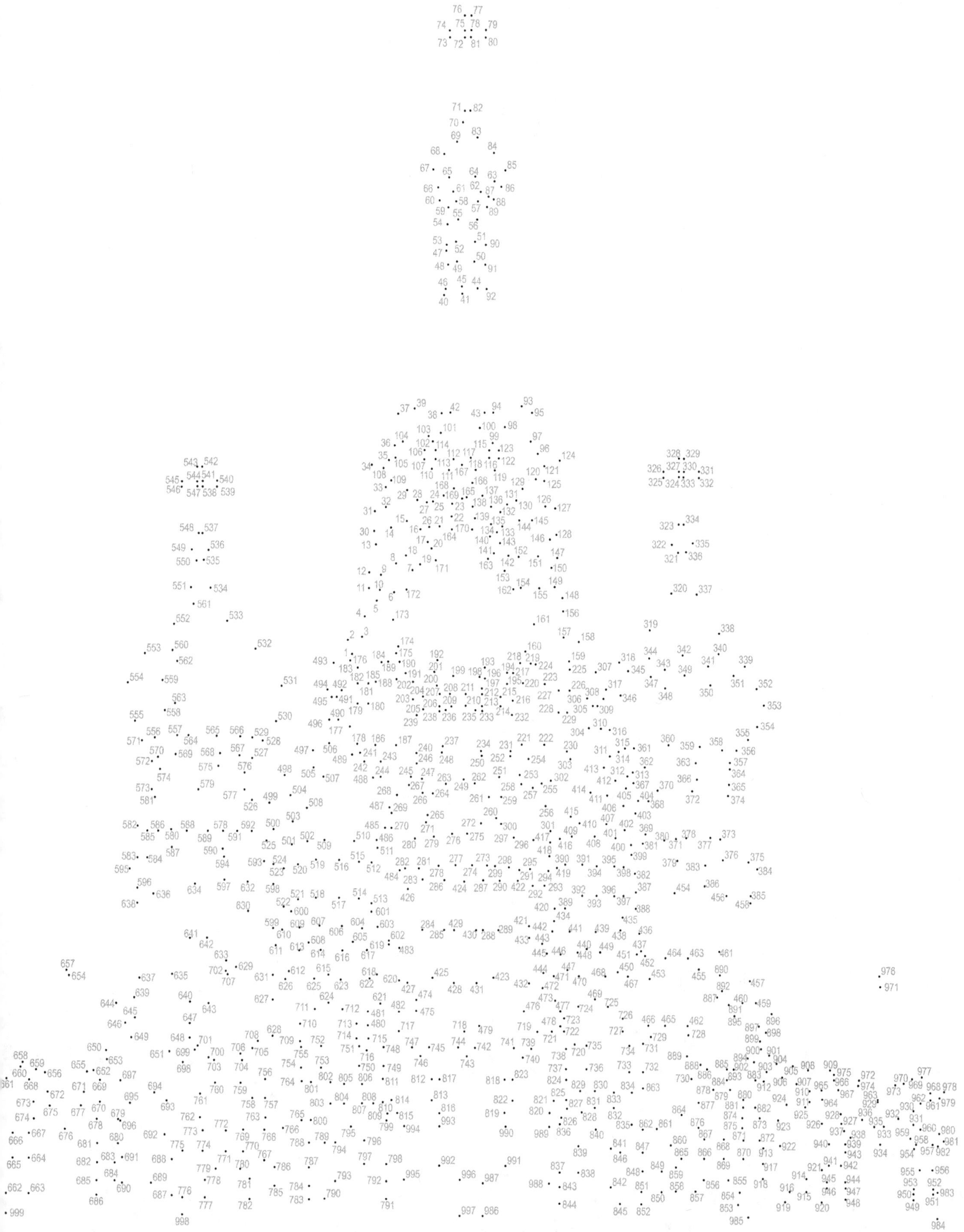

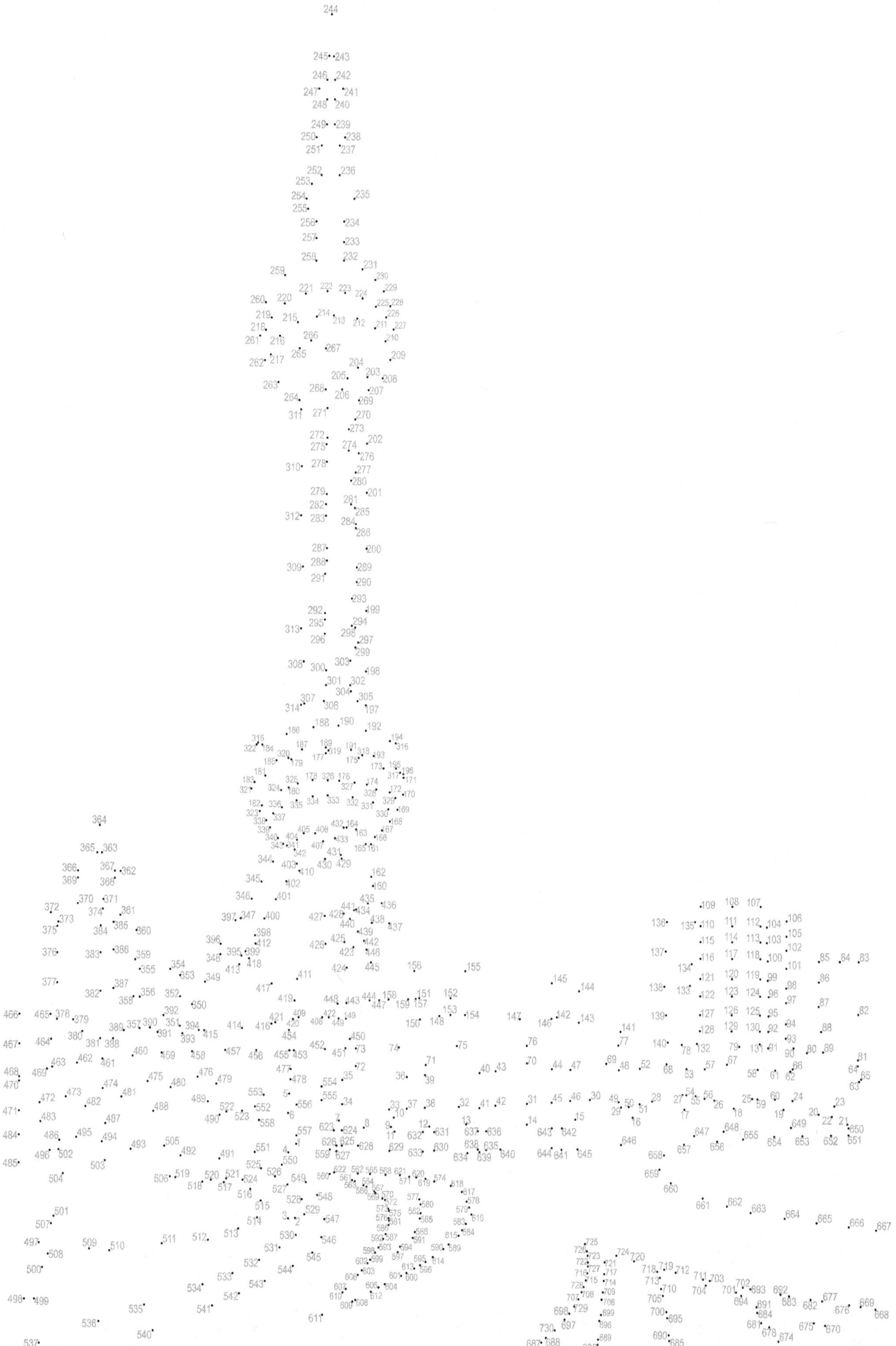

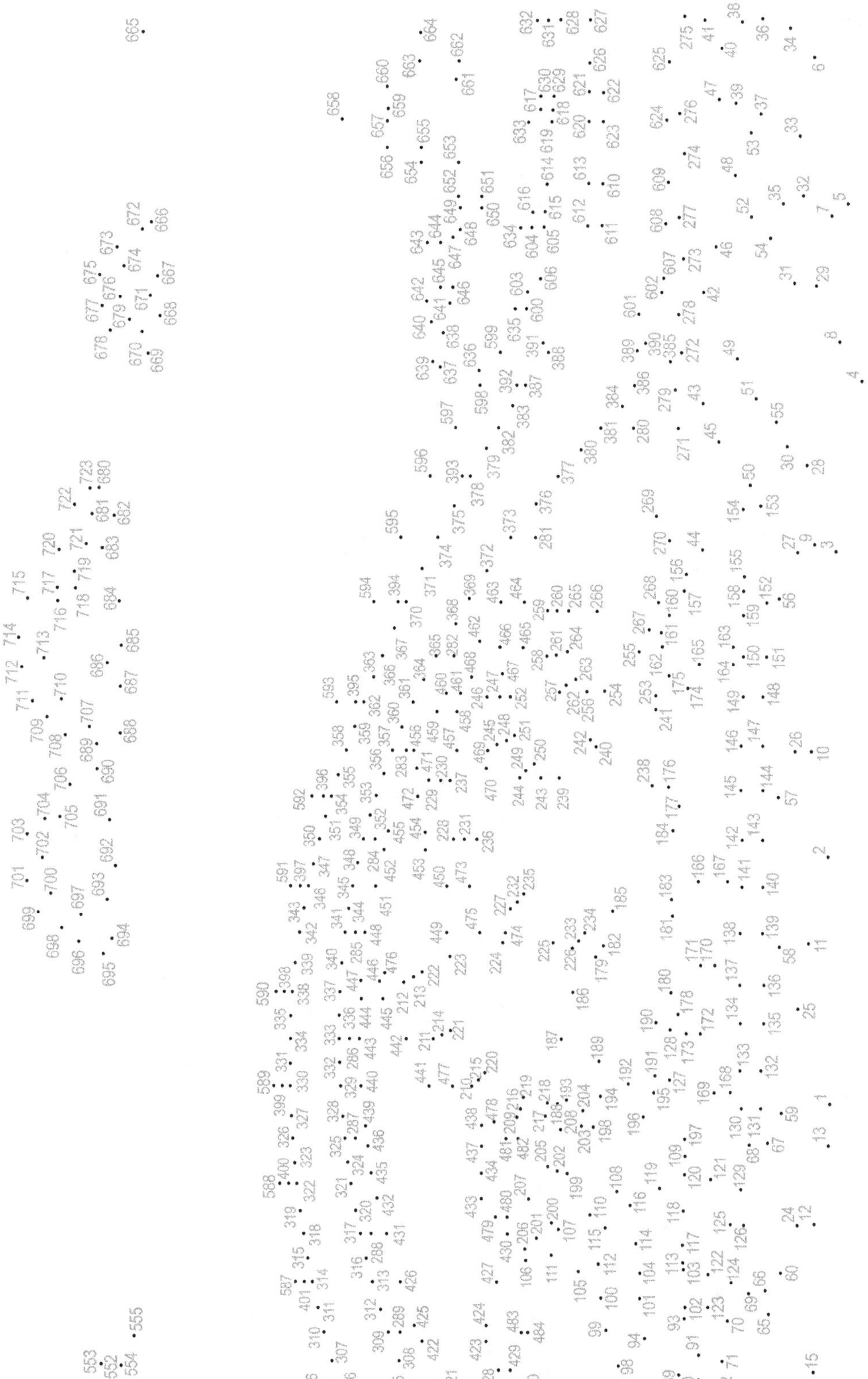

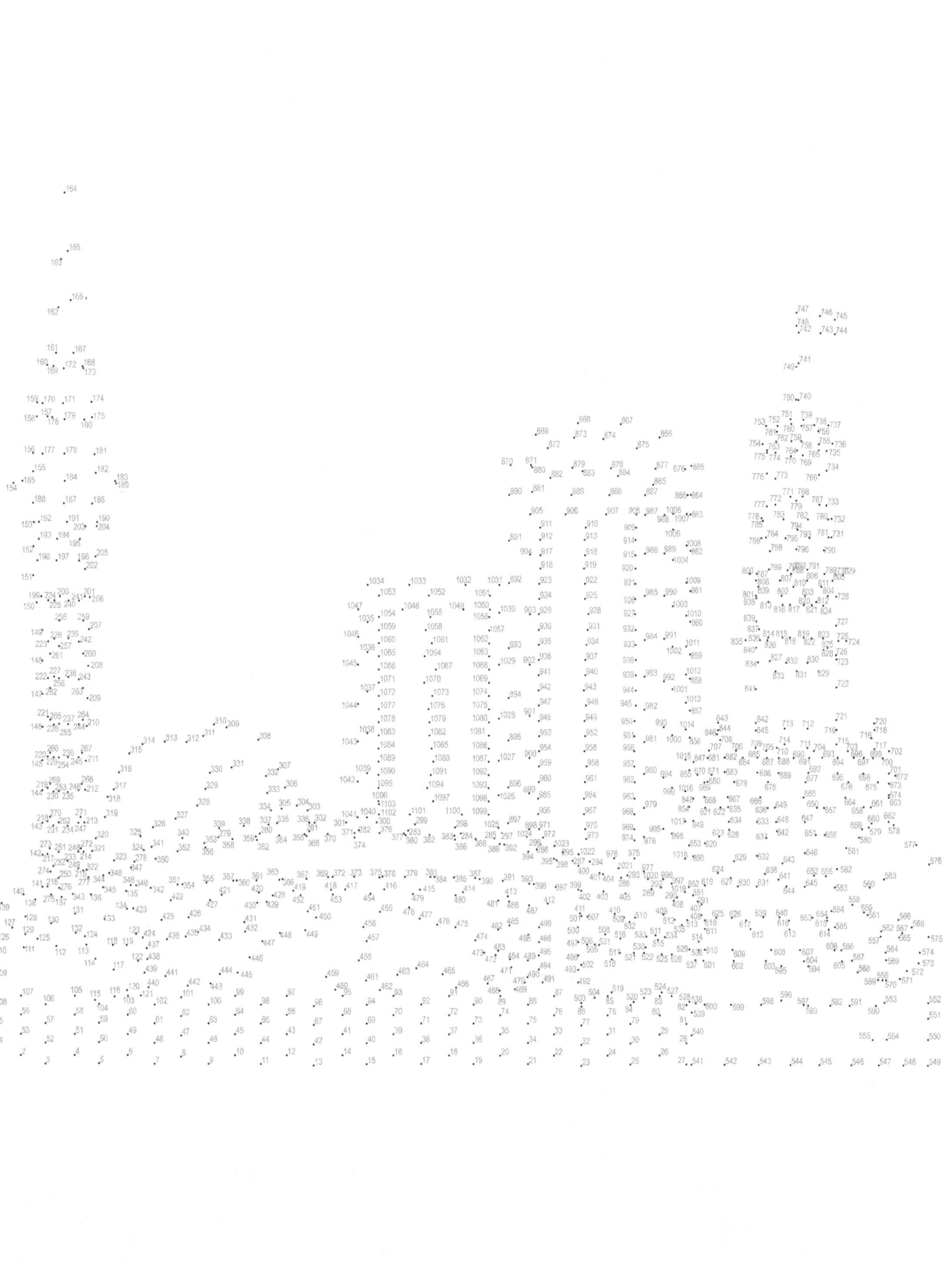

SOLUTIONS

Page 3: San Francisco, USA: Golden Gate Bridge

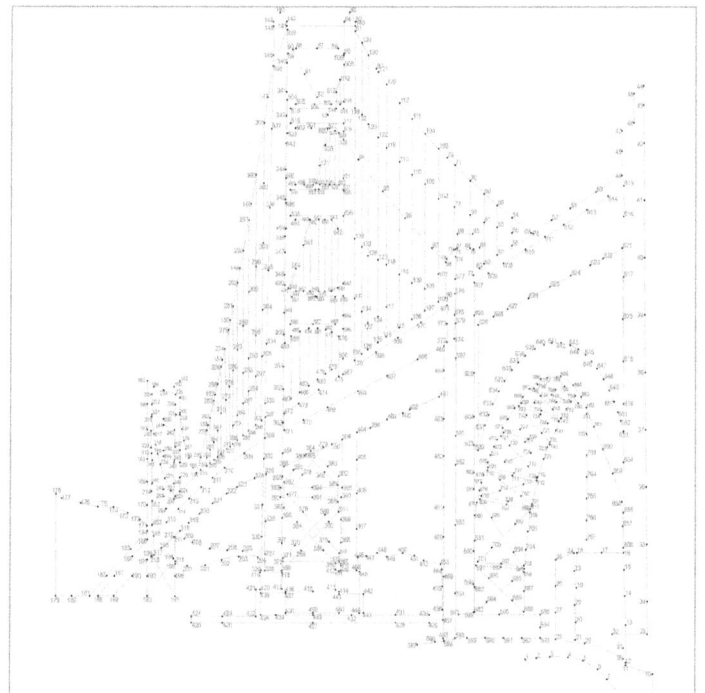

Page 5: Los Angeles, USA: Santa Monica Pier

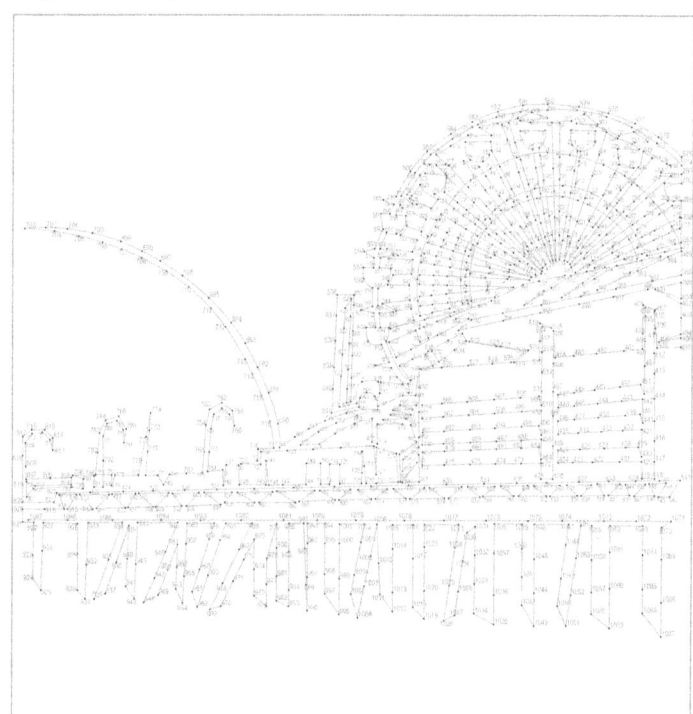

Page 7: Washington, USA: Lincoln Memorial

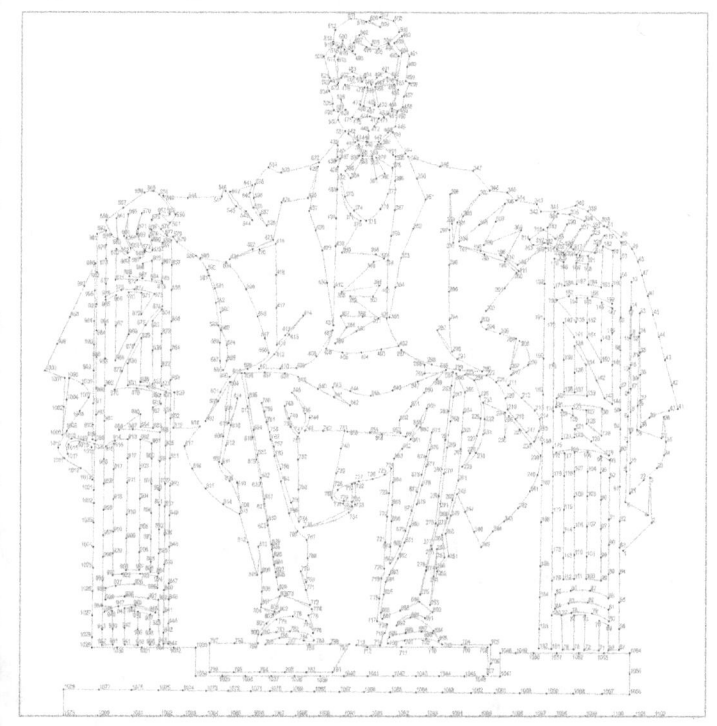

Page 9: New York, USA: Times Square

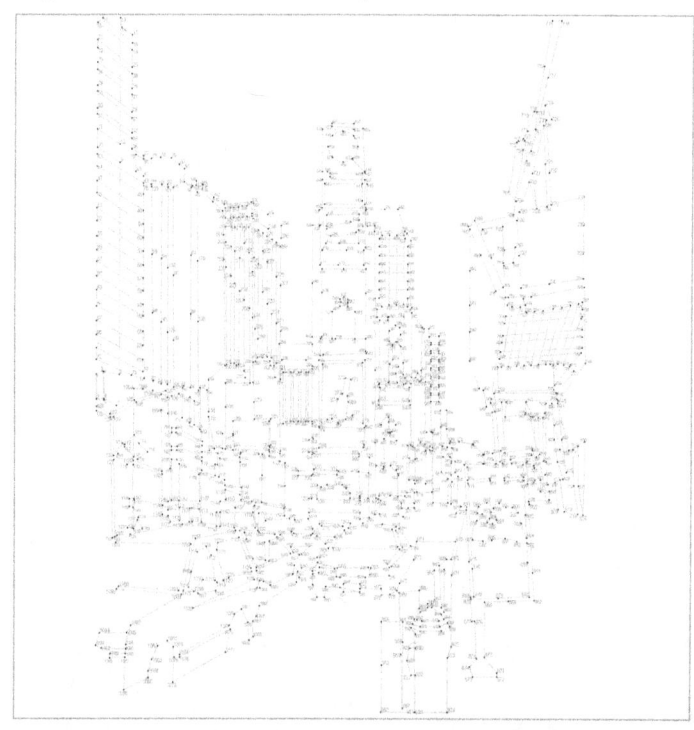

SOLUTIONS

Page 11: New York, USA: Empire State Building

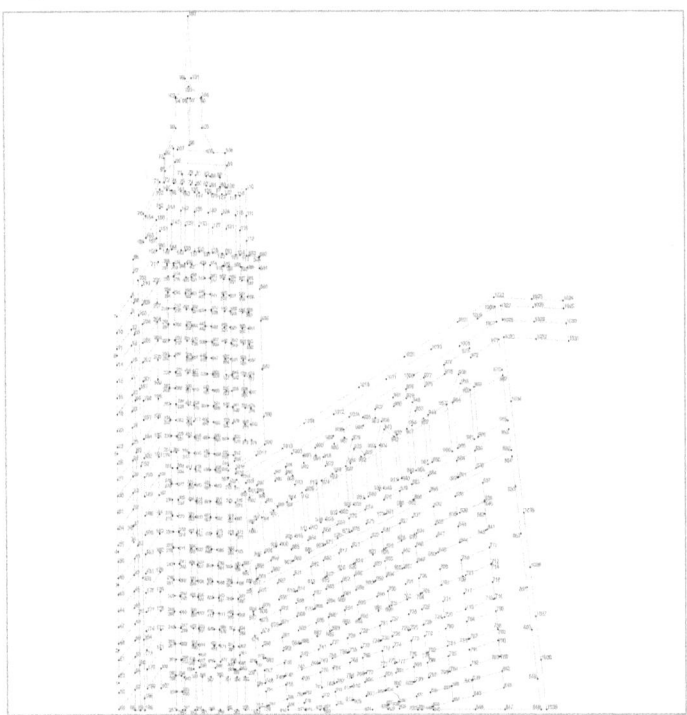

Page 13: Rio de Janeiro, Brazil: Christus Redentor

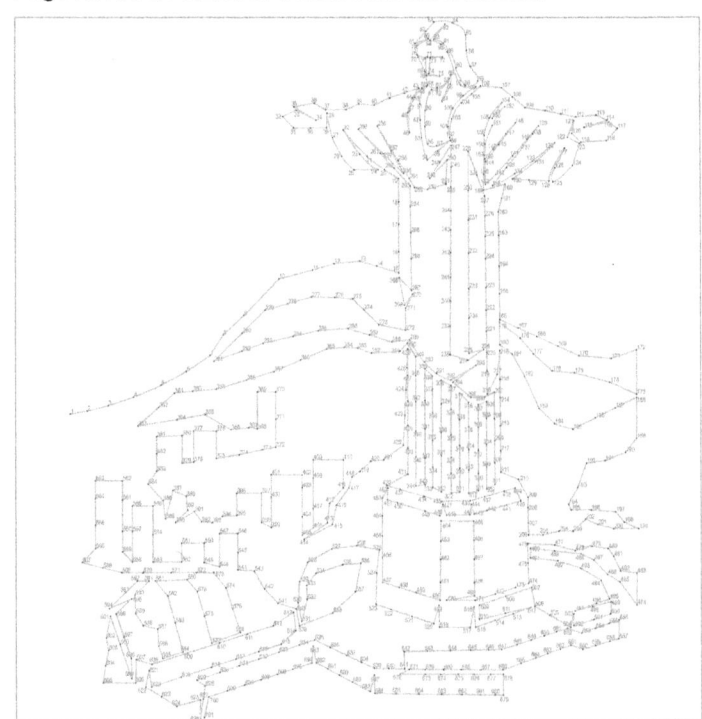

Page 15: Barcelona, Spain: Sagrada Familia

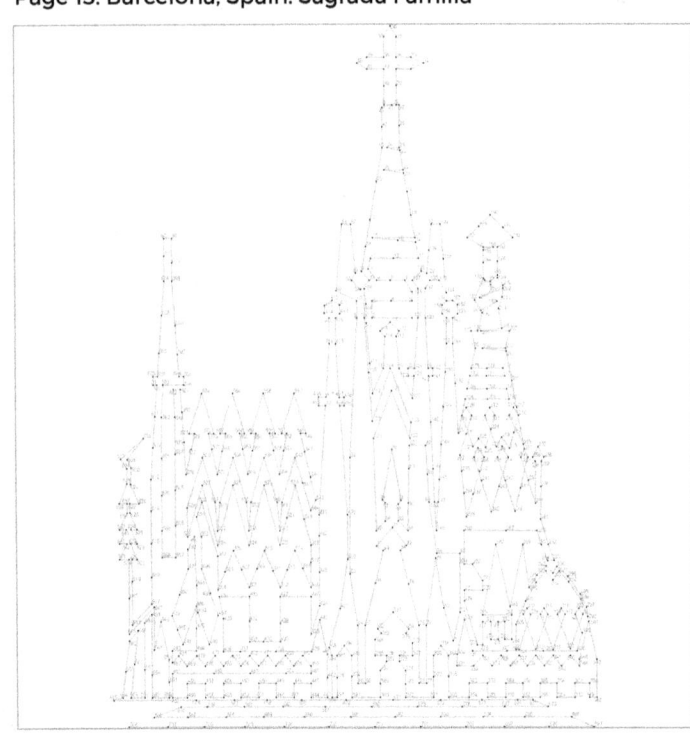

Page 17: London, England: Big Ben

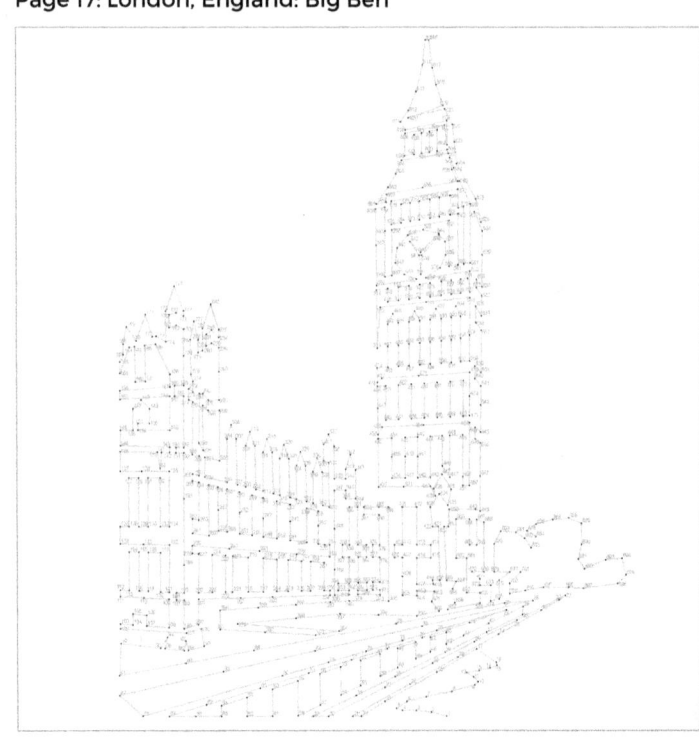

SOLUTIONS

Page 19: Paris, France: Eiffel Tower

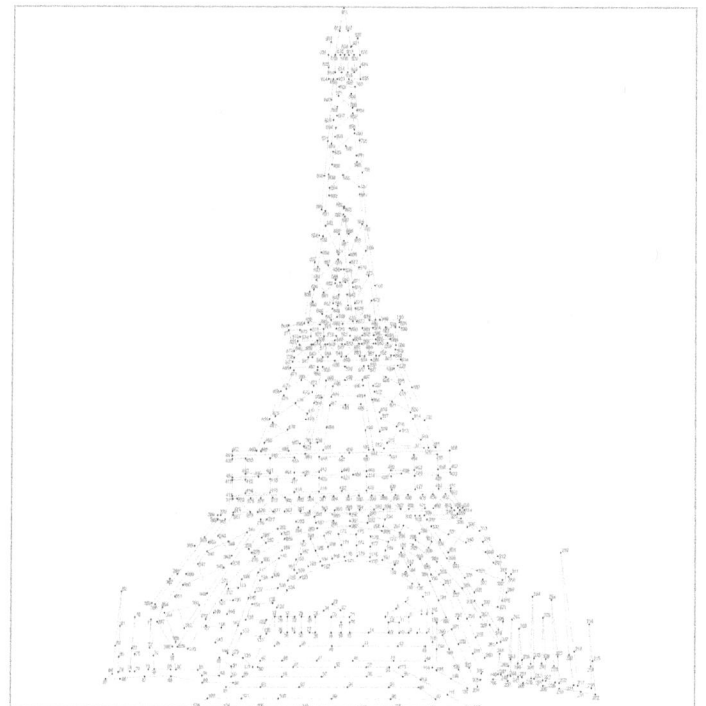

Page 21: Amsterdam, Netherlands

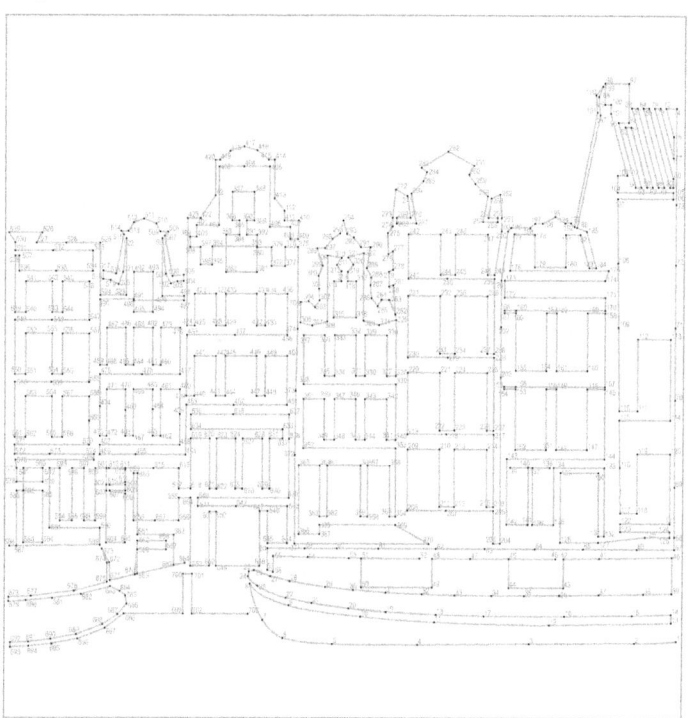

Page 23: Rome, Italy: Trevi Fountain

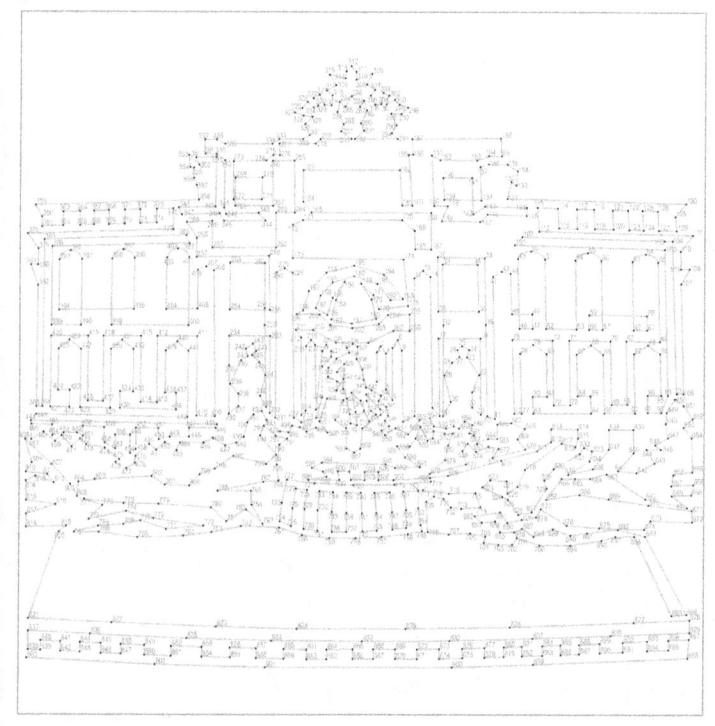

Page 25: Rome, Italy: Petersdom

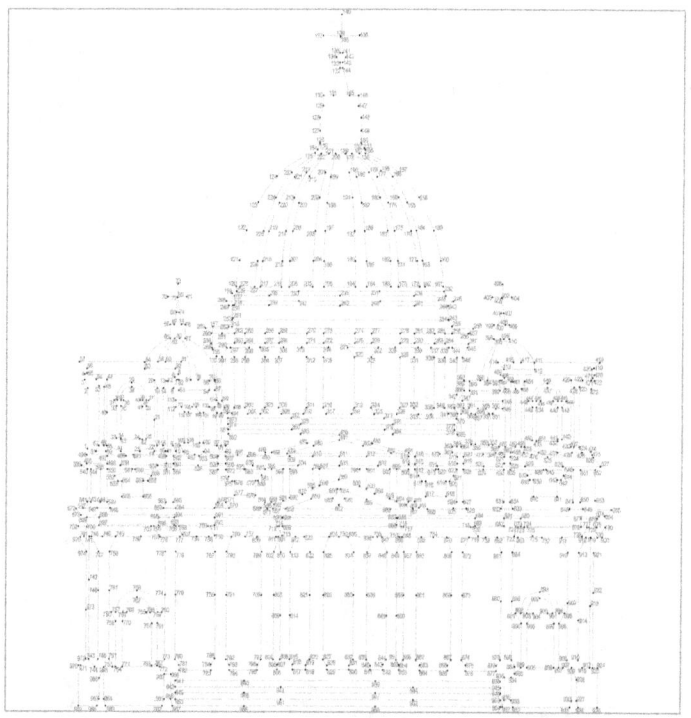

SOLUTIONS

Page 27: Florence, Italy: Ponte Vecchio

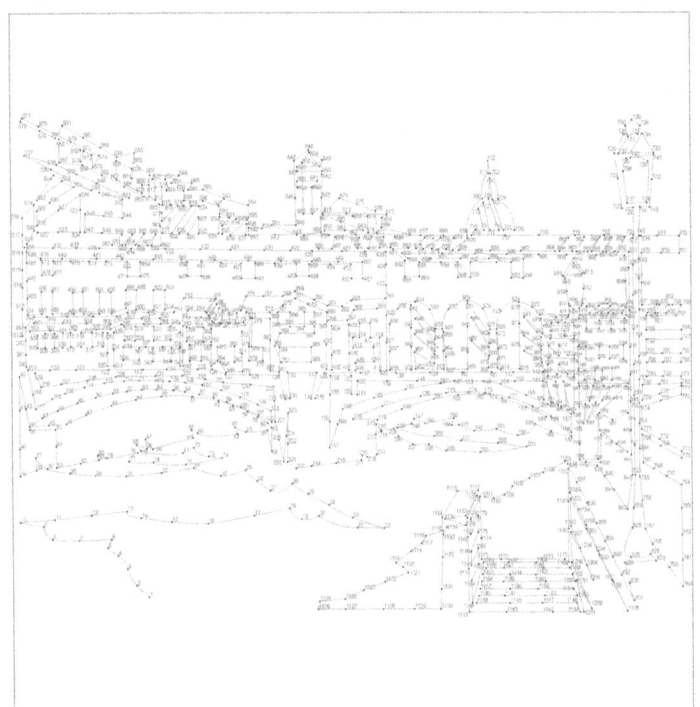

Page 29: Istanbul Turkey: Hagia Sophia

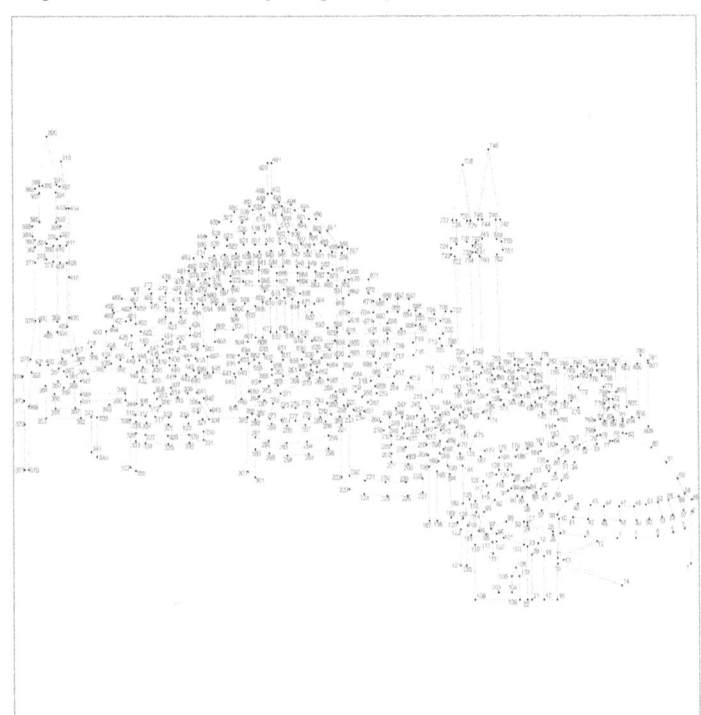

Page 31: Petra City, Jordan: The Treasury

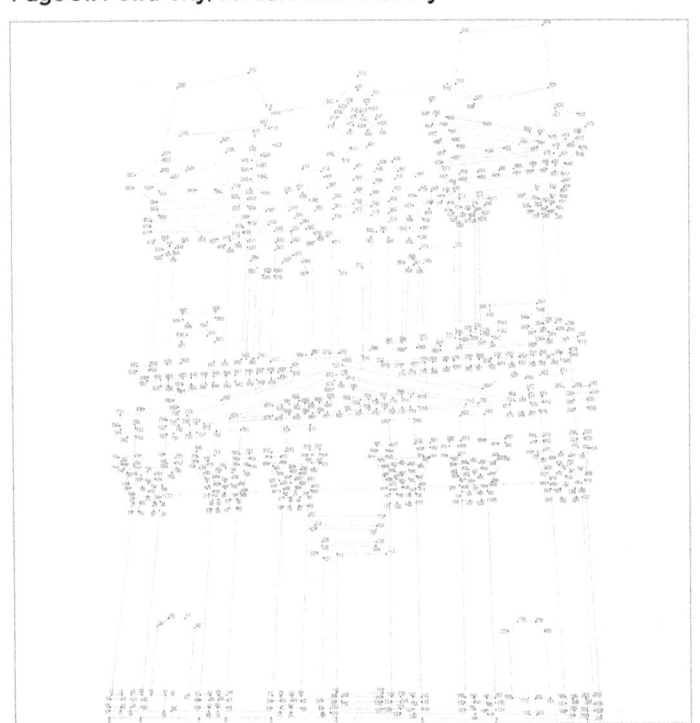

Page 33: Moscow, Russia: Saint Basil's Cathedral

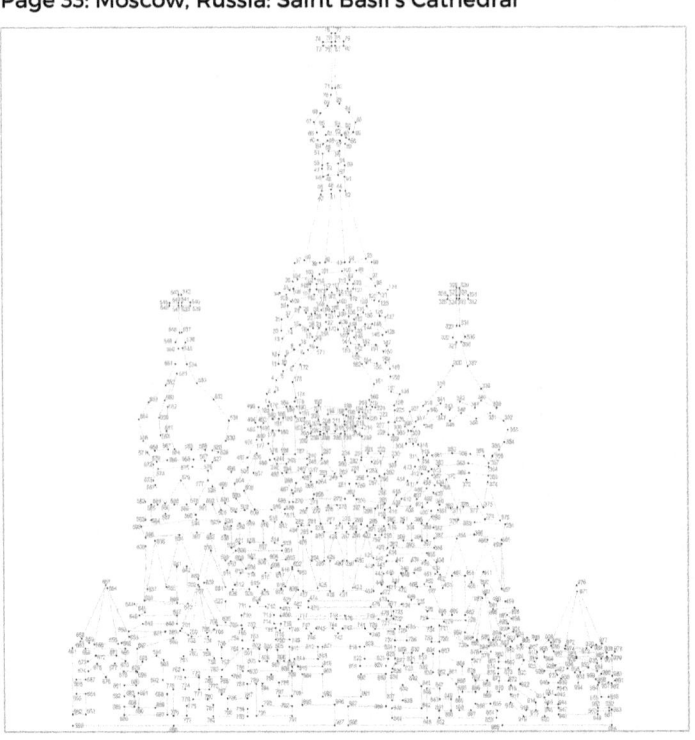

SOLUTIONS

Page 35: Shanghai, China: Pearl Tower

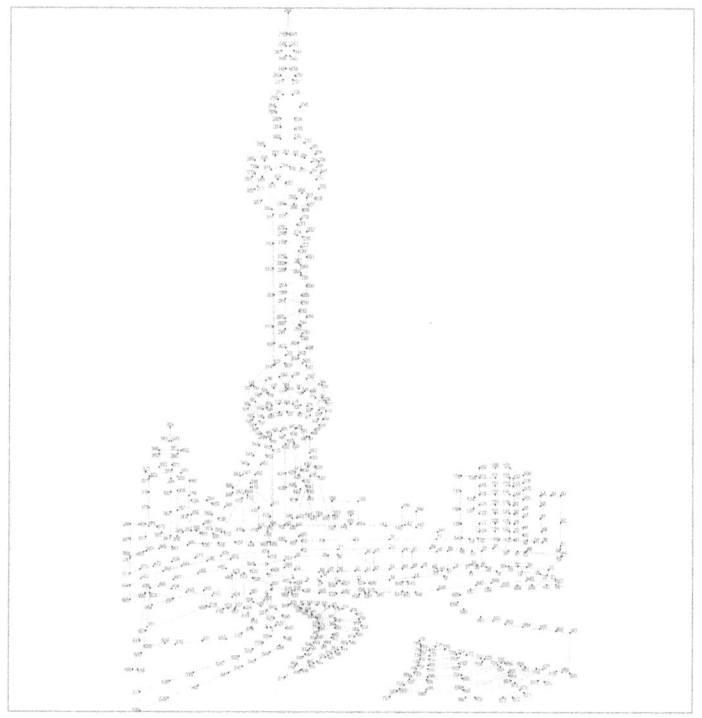

Page 37: Tokyo, Japan: Tower

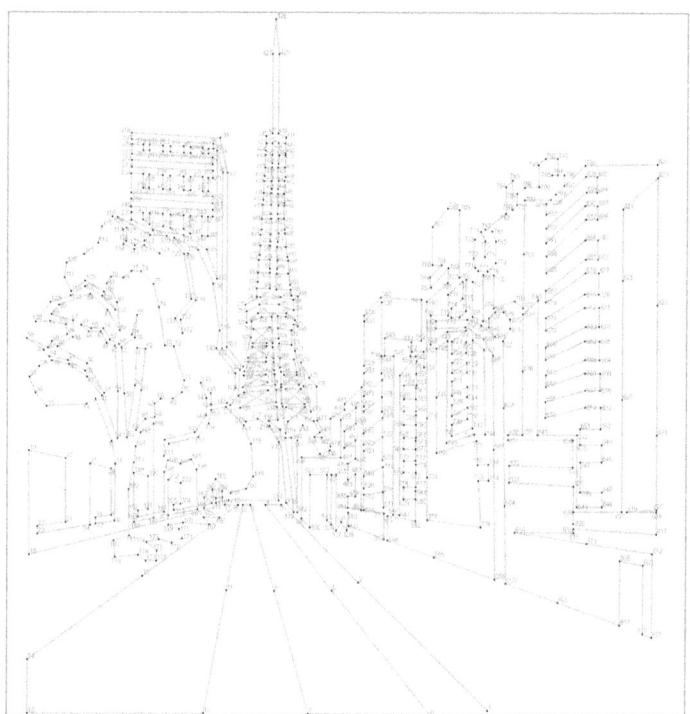

Page 39: Sydney, Australia: Opera House & Harbour Bridge

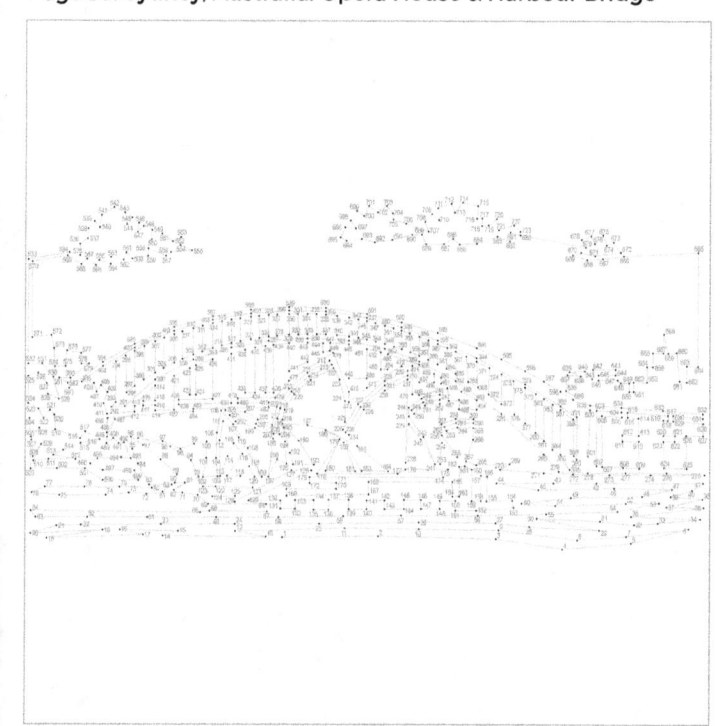

Page 41: Auckland, New Zealand: Skyline

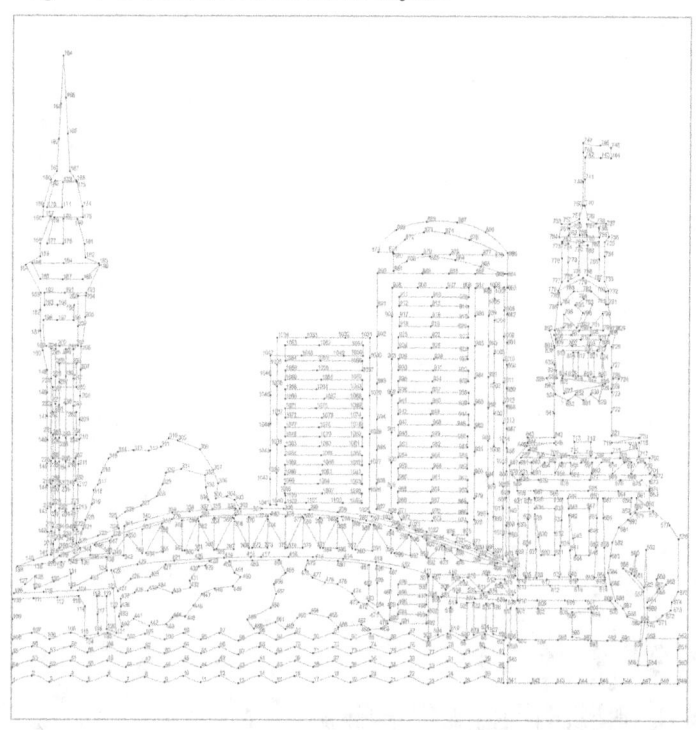

www.ingramcontent.com/pod-product-compliance
Lightning Source LLC
Chambersburg PA
CBHW082154230526
45467CB00044B/3365